Bernese Mountain Dog Training: The Beginner's Guide to Training Your Bernese Mountain Dog Puppy

Includes Potty Training, Sit, Stay, Fetch, Drop, Leash Training and Socialization Training

Brittany Boykin

CAC Publishing
ISBN: 978-1-948489-72-0
Brittany Boykin

Table of Contents

Table of Contents

Introduction

The Bernese Mountain Dog might not be as popular as breeds like Labrador Retrievers or Golden Retrievers, but Berner owners simply can't get enough of their lovable and fluffy companions. This classically beautiful breed is known for its amazing versatility coupled with extreme intelligence. A Bernese Mountain Dog is capable of assuming many different roles, including:

- Companion dog
- Family pet
- Herding dog
- Show dog
- Obedience dog
- Working dog
- Guide dog for the blind
- Hearing dog for the deaf
- Search and rescue dog
- Tracking dog
- Hunting dog
- TV actors
- … and many more

A Bernese Mountain Dog is characterized by its superior intelligence, high curiosity, boundless energy, versatility and regal good looks. These clever dogs can be very easy to train and can seem almost eager to learn new tricks and ways of pleasing their owners at very young ages.

However, as intelligent and easy to train as they may seem, there are times when some Bernese Mountain Dog owners may begin to feel frustrated and impatient when they don't see much success with their efforts. This can happen when your training methods don't take into consideration what's important to your dog and what makes him want to obey you the most.

Is a Bernese Mountain Dog Right for You?

As attractive a breed as the Bernese Mountain Dog might seem, it's important to remember they're not right for everyone. Due to their natural high intelligence and curiosity, these dogs need plenty of mental stimulation to keep them from becoming bored.

Bernese Mountain Dogs require plenty of exercise. Taking your dog out for walks regularly is important for more than just their physical health, your daily walk also provides him with some mental stimulation and some quality bonding time with his human.

This breed of dog is also capable of intense loyalty to his/her person, forming a life-long bond that is almost impossible to break. They'll love you unconditionally and want to do those things he thinks may please you most.

When a Bernese Mountain Dog forms a close bond with his human, he will think of a myriad of ways to try and get his human's attention – whether good or bad. This can mean he will pull laundry from the line or dig holes or chew your shoes if he believes that's the only way you'll focus your attention back on him again.

This kind of destructive behavior can become present in any breed of dog, but with a dog of high intelligence and a strong sense of family bonding, it's more important than ever to find ways to re-direct these instincts into more positive behaviors while your dog is still young.

Bernese Mountain Dogs crave companionship. To them, you and your family are his pack. They do not make good kennel dogs and won't respond well to being left alone in the back yard for long hours on end. This breed of dog is more likely to suffer from separation anxiety than some others if not taught early how to deal with you leaving for work.

If you don't have the time or the patience to offer a Bernese Mountain Dog the training, exercise and companionship it craves, then perhaps consider looking into a different breed of dog.

How Much Is Enough Exercise?

It's always sad to hear people say 'My dog doesn't need that much exercise. He seems happy to lie around at my feet all day.'

This is never a good reason to assume your dog doesn't need the mental and physical exercise – especially with a working breed like the Bernese Mountain Dog.

It's true that many Bernese Mountain Dogs seem at their happiest when they're allowed to curl up anywhere near their owner and will stay there for hours on end. In fact, I have a Bernese Mountain Dog curled up under my desk at my feet while I write at this very moment.

This is predominantly because a Bernese Mountain Dog will feel happy to be included in whatever you're doing, but it isn't enough for his physical health and well-being.

Walking

Your dog won't view being taken out for a walk as 'exercise time'. He views it as being invited out by the family pack for a 'hunt'. He knows he'll have the opportunity to look around for potential food, sniff around for other dogs or potential prey, and spend some quality time as part of the pack as well. For him, this constitutes mental stimulation as well.

Bernese Mountain Dogs will naturally travel in a cantering-lope rather than a slow walk. During your walks together, be sure you move at a brisk pace so your dog is able to trot alongside you in a comfortable gait for his size. This can mean walking quickly or even jogging to make sure you keep at the speed of his gait without him needing to pull ahead.

Walking is also great for keeping knee, hip and elbow joints supple in this large breed of dog. Many large breeds are known to suffer from hip problems later in life, so regular exercise can help to keep your beloved dog fit and healthy for much longer.

Play-Time

Bernese Mountain Dogs are naturally playful, inquisitive and curious. A bored dog can quickly become destructive as he looks for things to occupy his mind. This can mean digging holes in your garden, ripping laundry off the line, chewing your favorite shoes or barking out of sheer boredom.

Play-time is about giving him a bit of time to just be a bit silly and have some fun, but it's also an important time to reinforce the bond between you and your dog.

Play-time should be an important part of your dog's exercise routine and should be something your dog finds fun and entertaining. This can mean teaching your dog to fetch a ball or Frisbee and then throwing it around for him in the yard or at the park. Most Bernese Mountain Dogs love to play a game of tug-of-war, so find a suitable rope-toy and encourage him to play with you. This helps to strengthen shoulder and jaw muscles.

You can also incorporate games that stimulate his mind and his need to hunt, such as hide-and-seek. Bernese Mountain Dogs enjoy tracking down an owner who is hiding in a closet, behind a bush, around the side of the house or behind a door, so make it a fun game and praise him when he finds you.

Hunting

While Bernese Mountain Dogs love to spend some time hunting and tracking down potential prey, this does NOT mean you need to take your dog out to kill wild animals. It can mean giving him something in his own yard to track and hunt that is rewarding for him mentally and physically.

It's possible to give them a small taste of the 'hunt' when they're out on their daily walk, but try scattering a handful of kibble or biscuits across your yard and telling him to go and find them. He'll spend as long as it takes sniffing every one of them out.

Many dog owners use specifically made, non-toxic chew toys designed to hold kibble inside. Your dog will happily spend time trying to work out how to get the food out. Don't use sticky or wet food, or you may find you attract ants rather than entertaining your dog.

These simple games can help your dog learn to hunt down food rewards and track any hidden treats you might leave around.

Choosing a Bernese Mountain Dog Puppy

Bernese Mountain Dog puppies are cute, fluffy and so irresistible, it's easy to see why so many people choose these gorgeous pups as potential pets.

If you intend to show or breed your dog, then always choose a reputable breeder who is willing to give you the complete family lineage and registration papers. This can help you determine the most likely size, coat length, coloring and even temperament the litter is likely to display as dominant features.

With purebred Bernese Mountain Dogs, you should also ask about the medical histories of both the sire and the dam, as this breed can have hereditary medical and psychological issues to watch for.

These can include hip or joint dysplasia, arthritis, heart problems, higher risk of the potentially fatal 'canine bloat' (gastric dilatation or gastric digestive volvulus syndrome) and other serious genetic problems.

What most people forget is that these adorable puppies grow into large, powerful dogs very quickly so you could be dealing with a 75 pound dog with the mind and behavior of a playful, mischievous puppy.

It's at this point that many unprepared owners give up on their dog. They'll give away the naughty pup or leave him at a shelter rather than taking the time to train them properly to become the loyal, loving, intelligent dog they all have the potential to be.

For the best results, you should begin basic training the moment your puppy comes home for the first time.

Bernese Mountain Dog puppies are incredibly smart. They'll pick up simple commands very quickly and if you remember to interact with them in a language they understand, it's possible to show your puppy how to modify his own behavior to suit the family 'pack' rules even while he's still very young.

The key to training such intelligent breeds of dog is to have plenty of patience and learn to work with the praise and reward method. This is especially true with Bernese Mountain Dogs, who respond very well to praise.

Your dog will develop a strong sense of respect for you as you spend time working to teach him, train him and discipline him, to the point that he'll happily do as you command simply because he knows it pleases you, which pleases him in return.

You will also find that such high levels of intelligence can also come with equally high levels of stubbornness and the need to dominate. In dogs, domination isn't about aggression or violence. It's about trying to establish the pack order and your puppy will work on lots of ways to try and figure out where his position is in your family pack.

Bringing Puppy Home

Bringing your puppy home for the first time can be an exciting day for you – but it's a stressful, scary day for your new puppy. After all, he's had the comfort and company of 6 or 7 litter-mates, plus his mother, since the day he was born. Now all he has is an unfamiliar new pack.

A puppy might seem like he's enjoying play time immensely when he first arrives, but the moment he's left on his own, the sudden loneliness will remind him that his mother is missing and he has no litter-mates to cuddle up to for warmth and comfort.

This is where a conscientious owner will provide somewhere safe and reassuring for a new puppy to sleep and offer him a replacement litter-mate to help him feel safe. One of the easiest ways to do this is to buy or create a comfortable bed and give him an old stuffed toy that is a little larger than he is.

That old stuffed toy may start out as a replacement litter-mate, but may end up being your puppy's friend and play-mate as he grows up.

Puppy training also begins on that very first day home. This is where you establish ground rules for what's acceptable behavior and what's not. Potty training should also be a high priority right from the beginning.

While your pup might seem small and cute right now, he will grow into a large dog, so it's not wise to encourage him to jump, bite or get onto human furniture at any time. You should also never give your puppy anything of your own to play with or chew. Always provide his own toys and bedding and spend some time teaching him to seek out his own things rather than yours.

Always remember to curb any puppy behavior you wouldn't like to see in an adult dog. This way your Bernese Mountain Dog will grow up understanding what belongs to him and what belongs to you. He'll also have a healthy respect for the family-home rules very early on.

Speaking Your Dog's Language

A responsible Bernese Mountain Dog owner will always take time to learn how to communicate effectively with their dog. This means learning to speak in a language your dog will understand.

When you give a dog a command or talk to him, he doesn't actually listen to the words you say. Rather, he's responding to the tone of voice and the position of your body.

If you listen to your dog, you'll notice he has a range and variety of different barks, ranging from warning barks, happy barks, greeting yaps, growls, whines, whimpers, playful yips, attention seeking calls and excitable or playful barks. Each of these is tone-based and has a variety of lengths and meanings.

In order to encourage your dog to continue repeating an acceptable or pleasing behavior, praise him using a high-pitched, happy voice. You might even use an affectionate pat, or even a small food reward if you're especially happy with something he's done right, to reinforce that's he's done well and you're really pleased.

However, if he's being bad or doing something unacceptable, giving a short reprimand that sounds a little like a low growl, such as 'ah ah', will remind him of the little guttural growls his mother would make to scold him when he was naughty. He should stop doing whatever earned him that reprimand.

Yelling at a dog is never seen as scolding in dog language. Your dog will assume you're giving out the same warning barks that he is, or he will assume you're being aggressive at some threat he can't see or perceive. If you yell at a dog, you risk making him tense, but you won't be effectively disciplining him in any way. In fact, yelling at him could be making his bad behavior even worse.

A reassuring, loving tone of voice is fine for when your dog is having a goofy, affectionate moment with you, but giving this same reassurance during a time of stress or fear won't actually help your dog to feel better.

In fact, if you reassure a dog while he's feeling fear, such as through a thunderstorm, then he may interpret your kind words as being told he was right to be scared.

Offering your dog any kind of reward just for being cute gives him the impression that he doesn't have to obey your commands in order to get treats. After all, if he waits long enough, he knows you'll give him something to eat.

It's also wise to distinguish the difference between bribery and reward. Your dog should receive treats after he's done something to earn them. He shouldn't have to be shown a reward or bribed into behaving by waving a treat in front of his nose.

Always consider how your dog hears your tone of voice when you're working on training techniques, when you're scolding him, or when you're playing. Remember that treats are to be earned and you'll soon find your dog will understand what's expected of him much more easily.

Effective Discipline

Far too many people assume that in order to discipline a dog, they need to smack his nose or yell at him or tie him up alone in the yard or rub his nose in the mess he made.

The truth is, none of these tactics work as effective discipline for any breed of dog. In fact, you could be making his behavior even worse.

In order to administer effective forms of discipline, it's important to understand a little bit about dog-language and then modify your disciplinary measures to suit something your dog will understand. Keep in mind that a dog is happiest when he can make his pack-leader happy. Hopefully, he views you as his pack-leader.

Never hit any dog, for any reason. In dog language, this is seen as unprovoked aggression. He doesn't understand why you're lashing out and could develop an unhealthy sense of fear of you. That fear could quickly turn into depression, anxiety, aggression or other psychological issues as your dog tries to figure out why you're violent toward him when all he wanted to do was play with you.

Always remember, an adult Bernese Mountain Dog has teeth and powerful jaws that could easily crush every bone in your hand. He just chooses not to. As a dog, he usually has an unconditional love for his owner, regardless of how he's being treated.

If you've learned how to convey your pleasure with good actions, then you should already realize that your dog craves your approval, your attention and your affection. In order to show him that you're not pleased with something, simply ignore him for a few minutes. Turn your back on him, fold your arms across your chest and look away. In dog language, this is a severe reprimand.

When he modifies his own behavior and is doing the right thing, lavishly praise on him with a happy, high-pitched tone of voice. Give him an affectionate pat as you say 'good dog'. He'll quickly learn that you're happy when he behaves well and he receives none of the things he wants most when he's acting badly.

It's also possible to modify bad behavior into good behavior fairly easily. For example, if you catch your dog chewing something of yours, remove the offending item and give him a short 'ah ah' and then replace it with one of his own toys. Praise him for playing with his own toy and he'll soon get the idea.

Potty Training Your Bernese Mountain Dog

Potty training any dog should be relatively easy. With a little patience should only take a couple of days to get your puppy to understand that he needs to relieve himself outside, in a specific area of the yard, and never in the house.

If you use your knowledge of dog language to teach your puppy what's expected of him, you won't need to worry about crates or puppy pads or newspapers or other "potty training aids". Your dog is smart enough to figure out what's expected of him, if you explain it the right way.

Your first step is to create a routine where you take puppy outside at regular intervals. These should be immediately after he wakes up from a sleep or a nap, after eating, several times throughout the day and immediately before going to bed.

Once you're outside together, let your puppy roam around the yard at will. Don't say anything. Just wait patiently for him. The instant you notice your puppy getting into position to relieve himself, give a command, like 'go potty' or 'go pee'. Repeat this command while he's relieving himself.

When he's finished, praise him with an affectionate pat and tell him he's a good dog. At first, your puppy will be very confused. After all, why would you praise him for doing what comes naturally?

This is where you need to practice a little bit of patience. Naturally, a puppy who thinks he's going to be praise for going potty will immediately try to get your positive attention the same way again. The next time he feels the urge to go, he'll make sure he does it right in front of you. If you're on the rug or in the house, then this is where he'll go.

It's important not to yell at or scold him for doing his business. Instead, pick him up silently and take him outside to finish what he was doing. While you're out there, reinforce the command to 'go potty' or 'go pee' and then praise him for attempting it outside in the yard. Then go back inside and silently clean up the mess he's made. Don't make eye contact. Don't make a fuss. Just clean it up.

After only a couple of short days of this routine, your puppy will begin trying to attract your attention in order to be let outside to go potty. This means you need to be aware of the attention-seeking tactics he'll try. He might grab your hand or clothing with his teeth and pull. He might whine or bark. He might paw at you to follow him to the door. No matter what he tries, get up and let him out. Praise him well for going on his own and you'll soon find he never has the urge to go inside the house again.

Basic Obedience Training

Spending time training all breeds of dog is important, but Bernese Mountain Dogs seem to thrive on the challenge of learning new things and making their owner happy.

As these are such intelligent dogs, you should find that they're very easy to train. They catch on quickly to what's expected of them. If you're willing to learn how to communicate effectively with your dog, then you should find it even easier to teach your Bernese Mountain Dog to become a happy, well-behaved member of the family.

Always work on a positive reward system of training. This means offering your dog a form of reward for good behavior or for doing something you wanted him to do. The easiest way to teach your dog to comply with your commands is to begin with something he was already going to do.

Sit

Sitting is a natural position for your dog, so it's easy to teach him to sit when you want him to. Hold a treat just above his nose. He should automatically sit so he can tilt his head back a little further to get a better sniff at the treat.

The moment his bottom touches the ground, give him the command 'sit'. Then give him the treat and tell him 'good dog'. You might also give him an affectionate pat as well, to reinforce the reward.

After a few repeats of this basic command and following up with a reward, your dog will understand that the command 'sit' means he's likely to get a treat and a pat if he sits down. There's reward and pleasure in it for him when he obeys.

Once he understands very simple commands, you can begin to introduce more training commands. He will already understand that he will be rewarded when he does what you command, so he'll immediately try to do what makes you happy enough to give him that treat and more affection.

Drop

Teaching your dog to lie down on his stomach on command can be very useful. It's also quite an easy command to teach, as it's a natural position for your dog.

Begin by holding a treat above his nose and telling your dog to sit. When he sits, he'll be expecting a treat. Don't give it to him yet. Instead, lower the treat down towards his front feet and move it slightly forward. This will encourage your dog to lower his head to reach for the food.

Gently encourage him to drop down into a prone position on his stomach by giving a gentle nudge on his shoulders. Never push or force him into position. Once he's laying down, say 'drop' and give him the treat.

Repeat this exercise one or two times a day until your dog will happily drop on command.

Come (Recall)

Before you allow your dog to go anywhere without a leash, it's vitally important to teach him to come to you when he's called. This is called a 'recall'. Bernese Mountain Dogs are large dogs. While you might think your dog is quite harmless, strangers don't know your pet as well as you do and may become afraid or angry at an uncontrolled dog jumping all over them.

Your dog needs to understand that when you call him to you, it means good rewards and good attention. He won't want to return to your side if he thinks you're going to growl at him, yell or scold him, or punish him in any way.

Begin by taking your dog out into the park on a very long leash. If you've already trained your dog to heel while out on a walk, then give him a release command that lets him know it's okay to roam about without the need to heel. (There is a more in-depth chapter on Leash Training in a later section of this book).

When his attention is off you, say in a high-pitched, happy tone 'come'. Open your arms wide, as though you were greeting a long-lost friend for a hug, but don't bend down to his level. Remain standing upright.

If he comes to you right away, praise him and give him a treat for returning when called. However, if he ignores you, give the leash a gentle tug and repeat the command again until he obeys. When he arrives at your feet, encourage him to sit before you give him his reward.

The praise and reward part of this exercise are important, as your dog will need to know it's worth his while coming back to you when you call him. Repeat this exercise once or twice during your walks and slowly extend the distance you allow him to wander away from you before calling him.

Fetch

Not all dogs will fetch a ball automatically for their owners. Some dogs need to be encouraged to learn how to play in this manner. Of course, once your dog gets the idea, it becomes a very fun training exercise for him and for you.

A tennis ball is usually a good way to begin teaching your dog to fetch. Roll the ball along the ground and encourage him to chase it. As he reaches the ball, tell him 'fetch'. Once he's picked it up, praise him highly and give him plenty of affection. He'll work out very quickly that picking up the ball means good attention from you.

When he's comfortable chasing after the ball and picking it up, hold off from giving him his reward as the exercise isn't finished. Instead, call him to you and encourage him to return to you while still holding the ball. When he gets back to you, praise him happily for bringing it back.

Stay

Teaching your dog to stay in position while you complete something else can be an invaluable command. You might want your dog to sit and stay in the hallway away from the front door while you answer the doorbell, or to teach him to leave his food bowl alone until he's told it's okay to eat, or perhaps get him to understand not to leave the boundary of your yard. There are a number of reasons the stay command can be very useful.

It's also slightly harder to teach a dog to stay, as you'll be rewarding him for doing nothing at all. Some dogs are naturally inclined to follow you around, so they won't immediately understand why you would give him a treat for sitting down doing nothing.

To begin, hold a treat above his nose and tell your dog to sit. When he's sitting, he'll be waiting for his treat. Don't give it to him yet, as the exercise isn't finished.

In a firm voice, tell him to 'stay'. Raise your hand, palm out, fingers together, like a stop sign at the same time.

Take one confident step backwards, away from your dog. Repeat the command to stay. You want him to remain sitting until you tell him otherwise. Wait two or three seconds, repeat the command and the hand signal and then step back towards him again.

If he remained in position, give him his treat and some praise. Gradually increase the distance and the time you wait to return to him until he understands that you want him to just sit and do nothing until you get back with his reward.

Eventually, you should be able to make your dog understand that he will always get positive attention, praise and affection if he simply stays put when he's told. You should even be able to leave his direct line of sight and know that he'll still be sitting there waiting for you when you get back.

You should never call a dog to you after you've asked him to stay. You always return to him to release him from the command.

Wait

Teaching a dog to 'wait' is not the same command as teaching him to stay. It's also a little more difficult to get your dog to understand the difference between the two commands. While the dog is still expected to remain in the same spot until the exercise is finished, the difference between 'wait' and 'stay' is very important.

The 'wait' command becomes very important if you intend to continue your dog's training past the basic commands and into more advanced territory, such as agility work. It can also be very helpful if you need to cross busy streets while you're out walking, as you can ask him to wait at the curb before crossing.

When you ask a dog to wait, you want him to remain still until you call him to you. The exercise ends when he moves to you to get his praise. However, when you ask a dog to stay, you expect that he'll stay in position until you return to him. The exercise ends when you return and give him his praise.

Once he's effectively learned that a firm-voiced command of 'stay' means not to move, you need to work on adopting a different tone for the command to 'wait'.

Tell him to sit. Use a casual voice as you give the 'wait' command, with a warning finger raised to him. He'll notice the difference in tone and in hand signal, but won't immediately figure out why. Walk a few steps away from him and then give the happy command to 'come'. Encourage him to come to you.

At first, he will be very confused as to why he's allowed to move from his 'stay' position. Reinforce this lesson by giving him a very firm-voiced command to 'stay' with a stop-signal hand sign. Walk a few steps away, and then return to him before giving him his reward.

Now try the casual tone 'wait' command with one warning finger raised. He should still be in sitting position, so move several steps away before calling him to you.

Be patient when teaching your dog this subtle difference between commands and be sure you remain consistent in your tone and expectation. He'll soon pick up what you want him to do.

Leash Training Your Bernese Mountain Dog

Have you ever seen someone being dragged around
behind a dog on a leash? It's as though the dog is taking
the human for a walk, not the other way around. Dogs that
pull and strain at the leash and drag their owners around
have pack-leadership issues. They believe they're in
control of the 'hunt' and they don't have a clear
understanding of who the real leader of the pack is.

An adult Bernese Mountain Dog can be very powerful. The
last thing you need is a strong dog that you can't control
effectively during a walk, so it's important to begin leash
training at a very young age.

During your walks, your dog needs to understand when you want him to walk at 'heel', or remain with his nose by your left knee, and when it's okay for him to roam a little and sniff things. Before you get to that stage, though, you must first teach him that walking at heel is the right position to be in unless you tell him otherwise.

The Right Leash and Collar

Never buy leashes or collars that are too big for your dog. As Bernese Mountain Dogs grow very quickly, this can mean you need to buy several new collars as he grows out of the smaller ones, but you'll find his training will be much easier if you choose the correct size and fitting for whatever size he is at that time.

Leash Training a Very Young Puppy

Many dog trainers advocate attaching a leash to your dog's collar to get him used to having it there for a short while each day for a week or two. While this might work for some breeds of dog, a Bernese Mountain Dog is intelligent enough even at 8 weeks old to know what the leash means within a few minutes of going out for his first walk.

Your puppy's first walk with you should be an undirected, patient stroll around the front yard or even just one or two houses along the street. Your aim with this is to teach the puppy that having a collar on and being attached to a leash means he gets to follow you around and see new, strange things without anything bad happening to him. At first, he'll have no idea what's going on, so take a few steps and encourage him to follow you.

Never tug at the leash and never allow it to get tight. Don't drag your puppy anywhere, or he may develop a fear of the collar and leash. Simply encourage him with your voice to follow you while you walk a short distance.

If your puppy decides it's all so exciting and begins to run ahead of you, don't ever tug at the leash to pull him back to you. Simply encourage him to come back to you by calling him.

Don't walk too long with a very young puppy. Simply let him get the idea that you're out and he gets to smell exciting new things, as long as he follows where you're going. Praise him when he trots along faithfully behind you. He'll learn quickly.

Leash Training a Boisterous Puppy

All Bernese Mountain Dog puppies are naturally curious and playful by nature. Once he begins to understand that going out for a walk means a bit of excitement and fun, he'll naturally begin to pull away from you to reach the good smells faster. You may also find that as he gets older, he'll begin testing your authority and pack leadership a little, which can also be a reason for pulling ahead. This is where you can begin some serious leash-training techniques.

The easiest way to regain control of a dog who is pulling away from you is to change direction sharply. Don't yell at your dog or scold him for pulling away. Simply turn in the opposite direction to where he's pulling and give the high-pitched, happy command 'watching'.

This tells your dog that he's not in trouble, but he should pay attention because you've changed direction. Your dog will look up at the happy command you've given and realize you've changed direction. He should run to catch up with you

When your dog has caught up and is walking alongside you, give the command to 'heel'. Take one or two steps and if your dog is still beside you, praise him for being there.

At first, he won't understand why you're praising him for simply walking, so he'll immediately try to pull away and walk in front of you. Give a short, growling 'ah ah', then change direction again, saying 'watching' in a happy voice.

Once again, your dog should run to catch up with you. Repeat the command 'heel' the moment he's walking at your side and praise him when he remains there. The longer he remains at your knee, continue giving encouraging words of praise.

Meeting Other Dogs and People

As you walk around with your dog, you're likely to encounter other people and other dogs. Many dogs will bark or growl at approaching dogs. Some dogs get so excited by the idea of meeting a new playmate that they'll yip excitedly and begin to pull at the lead to go and say hello.

Other dogs will even raise their hackles menacingly. This is usually a warning sign based out of fear that the strange dog may pose a threat to you and/or him, so he's displaying a warning to the other dog not to approach.

Your dog needs to understand that these strange people and animals are not threatening or dangerous to him or you. They are also not exciting new playmates – not until he's more in control of his behavior and reactions.

If your dog is likely to become excitable at the sight of new people or dogs approaching, tell him to sit before he notices the distraction before him. Praise him for being calm and wait quietly beside him until the distraction approaches. As they get closer, reassure your dog with a happy voice. It doesn't matter what you say to him – your tone is important here.

If the people look nervous around a large, barking dog, tell him words of encouragement that the people can hear. This has the effect of helping to calm your dog, but also helps to reassure the strangers too. Say something like "they're not scary people. You're a good dog. I know it's exciting, but sit down now. Be a good boy."

You're actively diffusing all the exciting parts of being near new people or strange dogs and distracting him long enough to realize that there was no threat involved. There was no playing or interacting involved. In fact, the whole encounter was quite boring. Your dog will learn quickly that there's no need to bark or growl or yip next time.

Socializing Your Bernese Mountain Dog

Most Bernese Mountain Dogs are extremely loyal to their 'pack'. Once they have an understanding of who's part of the pack and what pecking order has been established, they'll consider themselves part of it.

However, you may also find that this pack instinct can translate to a mistrust of people or dogs they consider to be from other packs.

Socializing your dog with other people and other dogs is extremely important. Your dog needs to understand how to behave around strangers and around unfamiliar dogs without becoming aggressive or overly protective of you.

Please be aware that socializing does not necessarily mean taking your dog for a play-date with every other dog in the neighborhood at the doggy park. This is a human concept and not one that is familiar to most dogs. Not all dogs will be happy to mingle with strange dogs they view as being from a rival pack.

Effective socializing means getting your dog familiar with meeting new people, and teaching him how to react when he meets new dogs.

The easiest way to introduce your Bernese Mountain Dog to a myriad of new dogs and people is to enroll in a puppy class. In a group class, your puppy will have an opportunity to mingle with all kinds of new friends. This can help to teach him that dogs from 'rival packs' aren't a threat to him or to you, and will help prevent him from developing aggressive behavior as he gets older.

How to Stop The Biting and Chewing

A Bernese Mountain Dog will grow to have extremely powerful teeth and jaws. All puppies will chew to help support and develop jaw strength.

Always remember, chewing is a natural behavior, so trying to stop it completely just won't work. However, it is possible to re-direct your dog's chewing attempts into more positive areas.

This means teaching your dog what is acceptable to chew and what's not. This simple lesson means your dog will always have the ability to chew when he needs to, without ruining your favorite shoes or furniture.

The best way to teach your dog to chew appropriate items and leave your things alone is to provide him with non-toxic dog chew-toys. These could be rubber or rope or novelty shaped – it doesn't matter. Just be sure his toys are safe for him. Avoid small parts or sticks that could harm gums or internal organs. What is important is that your dog understands his toys are his own.

The next time you catch your dog chewing on something that doesn't belong to him, don't scold him. Simply remove the item silently and replace it with one of his own toys. Don't ever scold a dog for displaying a natural behavior. Instead, show him how he can still do it with a positive outcome.

When he picks up his own toy and focuses on it, praise him highly. Spend a little time playing with the toy with him so he understands the positive association of chewing his own toy.

After a little persistence, you'll soon find that any time your dog wants attention, or wants to play, or just wants to chew, he'll automatically pick up his own toys and leave your things alone.

Biting

If you spend a little time watching a litter of puppies playing, you'll notice they bite each other as part of their play. While this might look cute when they're young, as a Bernese Mountain Dog puppy grows, his teeth and jaws become more powerful, and it's no longer so much fun.

Along with play-biting, some dogs also 'mouth' their owners. This is actually a display of affection in some cases, and an attempt to seek attention in others. Once again, this is considered inappropriate behavior in an adult dog, especially if you have guests or visitors over.

Once again, you will need to spend some time showing your dog how to play-bite on a positive level. This is where his own non-toxic chew toys can become his way of showing you affection and seeking attention in a positive way.

When you notice your dog is mouthing you or biting at your hands or arms playfully give him a sharp 'ah ah' reprimand and remove your hand. Then encourage him to grab his chew toy instead and spend some time playing with him to reinforce the positive connotations of biting an acceptable object rather than your hand.

Advanced Training Techniques

Bernese Mountain Dogs thrive on challenges. Their high intelligence level means they will relish the idea of more difficult training tasks. This makes the Bernese Mountain Dog an excellent breed for trial and agility work. As long as they realize there's a reward, some fun and some praise in it for them at the end of the task, they'll work hard to get it right.

The same principles of positive reward training apply with more advanced training techniques as with any basic training. However, the biggest difficulty is getting your dog to understand what's expected of him throughout each exercise in the first place.

There are plenty of advanced training tricks you can work on with your dog that stem from the most basic lessons he learned as a puppy. You might decide to train your dog to pick up his own toys and put them in a toy box when he's finished playing. You could decide to let your dog fetch the newspaper from the front yard for you every morning.

Or you might decide to enroll him in an agility training course to help keep him active and stimulated.

It's important not to start agility training or any advanced training that involves jumping until after your dog is older than 18 months old. Young bones need time to strengthen and develop properly. This will help to avoid injuries that may affect your dog's health later in life.

You should also be sure your dog understand and obeys the basic commands to sit, drop, go left and right, wait and come to you when he's called.

Most dog training classes will have an obstacle course for agility work available. If you're able to enroll in a dog class for basic training, you should be able to continue your dog's training through the regular grades and on into the more advanced grades.

Of course, you can get your dog used to the hurdles and obstacles by building a small agility course at home in the back yard. You can use a low bench as a hurdle and some cones placed around the yard as an obstacle course.

To begin, tell your dog to sit on one side of the hurdle. Once he's sitting, tell him to wait and move around to the other side of the hurdle. Show him you have a treat or favorite toy of his and call him to you, encouraging him to jump over the hurdle to get to you.

As he jumps, say 'over' or 'jump' and praise him highly when he reaches you. He'll soon get the idea that jumping over the hurdle means good rewards.

Try throwing a ball over the hurdle and get him to fetch it. At first, he'll run around the hurdle to get the ball, but encourage him to jump over it to go and get it, and jump over it again as he brings it back to you. He'll begin to understand it's a part of a game and plenty of fun – especially if he's getting plenty of positive attention for his actions.

Conclusion

A Bernese Mountain Dog is a truly delightful breed of dog. Aside from being classically beautiful dogs, they are highly intelligent, versatile, easily trained, loving, loyal, curious, playful and they make wonderful companions.

Many Bernese Mountain Dog owners are familiar with the quizzical sideways-head turn and the look of sheer intelligence in their eyes as they try hard to grasp what you're saying to them. Their quirky, inquisitive nature means they can be a lot of fun when they play or when they just want to be a little goofy with you.

It's unfortunate that some people seem afraid of these gentle giants. Negative impressions are formed through fear, usually after meeting a badly-trained or completely untrained dog with no control. A poorly trained Bernese Mountain Dog may become confused and a little difficult to handle, but with the right attention and discipline it can become a great family pet.

Always take time out of your busy day to spend some quality time together with your dog, either playing or just being goofy. Daily walks are essential with this breed of dog, for both mental and physical stimulation. Grooming should also form an important part of his care and can help to strengthen the bond with you if you treat his grooming sessions as a big affection-giving session.

No matter how busy you are or what excuse you think of not to give your dog the things he needs, remember this: You have the TV, your computer, your work, your friends, the phone and a myriad of other things to keep you stimulated.

Your dog has only you.

Be all you can be for him. Spend time forging a bond with your Bernese Mountain Dog that consists of love, trust and understanding and you'll have a best friend for life.

If you enjoyed this book and picked up some awesome training tips, I would be sincerely grateful if you could leave a review on Amazon. Reviews are the best way to help your fellow readers sort through the nonsense so make sure to help them out! Leave A Review

If you're interested in learning more about potty training your puppy make sure to check out my new book titled 'Not in the House!'

Manufactured by Amazon.ca
Bolton, ON

30505145R00035